Cool Construction Vehicles

Kelley MacAulay and Bobbie Kalman

Crabtree Publishing Company

www.crabtreebooks.com

Created by Bobbie Kalman

Dedicated by Nancy Johnson
To Rich, for your love of construction,
as well as your ability to put a roof on a barn and a smile on my face.

Editor-in-Chief
Bobbie Kalman

Writing team
Kelley MacAulay
Bobbie Kalman

Substantive editor
Kathryn Smithyman

Editors
Molly Aloian
Michael Hodge

Photo research
Crystal Foxton

Design
Margaret Amy Salter

Production coordinator
Heather Fitzpatrick

Prepress technician
Nancy Johnson

Consultant
Tim Cruickshanks, president, Cruickshanks Property Services

Illustrations
David Carson: back cover, pages 8, 9, 10 (right), 12, 15, 16, 18, 20, 25, 26, 31,
    32 (all except compactor and dump truck)
Tammy Everts: pages 10 (left), 13, 32 (dump truck)
Katherine Kantor: page 32 (compactor)
Margaret Amy Salter: page 11

Photographs
Thomas Mayer/Alpha Presse: page 30
Photo courtesy of constructionphotographs.com: page 13
Construction Photography: page 27
© George Steinmetz/Corbis: pages 16-17
Dreamstime.com: © Darryl Brooks: page 18; © Roman Milert: page 31;
    © Robert Pernell: pages 6-7, 28; © Ernest Prim: page 4; © Liz Van Steenburgh: page 9
Fotolia.com: Vladimir Georgievskiy: page 3
Sherwood Hoffman/Index Stock: front cover (bulldozer)
iStockphoto.com: pages 5, 11, 12, 24, 26, 29
Katherine Kantor: page 15
Diane Payton Majumdar: page 8
© ShutterStock.com: Florin C: page 23; Titus Manea: page 14; Roman Milert: pages 20-21;
    Roger Dale Pleis: page 22; Francois Etienne du Plessis: pages 19, 25;
    Jason Smith: page 7; Brad Whitsitt: page 1
Other images by Corel

Library and Archives Canada Cataloguing in Publication

MacAulay, Kelley
    Cool construction vehicles / Kelley MacAulay & Bobbie Kalman.

(Vehicles on the move)
Includes index.
ISBN 978-0-7787-3042-2 (bound)
ISBN 978-0-7787-3056-9 (pbk.)

    1. Earthmoving machinery--Juvenile literature. 2. Cranes, derricks, etc.
--Juvenile literature. I. Kalman, Bobbie, 1947- II. Title. III. Series.

TA735.M33 2007   j629.225   C2007-900588-8

Library of Congress Cataloging-in-Publication Data

MacAulay, Kelley.
Cool construction vehicles / Kelley MacAulay & Bobbie Kalman.
    p. cm. -- (Vehicles on the move)
Includes index.
ISBN-13: 978-0-7787-3042-2 (rlb)
ISBN-10: 0-7787-3042-5 (rlb)
ISBN-13: 978-0-7787-3056-9 (pb)
ISBN-10: 0-7787-3056-5 (pb)
    1. Earthmoving machinery--Juvenile literature. 2. Construction
equipment--Juvenile literature. I. Kalman, Bobbie. II. Title. III. Series.
TA725.M43 2007
629.225--dc22
                                                        2007002695

Crabtree Publishing Company
www.crabtreebooks.com   1-800-387-7650
Copyright © **2007 CRABTREE PUBLISHING COMPANY**. All rights reserved. No part of this publication may be reproduced, stored in a retrieval system or be transmitted in any form or by any means, electronic, mechanical, photocopying, recording, or otherwise, without the prior written permission of Crabtree Publishing Company. In Canada: We acknowledge the financial support of the Government of Canada through the Book Publishing Industry Development Program (BPIDP) for our publishing activities.

Published in Canada
Crabtree Publishing
616 Welland Ave.
St. Catharines, ON
L2M 5V6

Published in the United States
Crabtree Publishing
PMB16A
350 Fifth Ave., Suite 3308
New York, NY 10118

Published in the United Kingdom
Crabtree Publishing
White Cross Mills
High Town, Lancaster
LA1 4XS

Published in Australia
Crabtree Publishing
386 Mt. Alexander Rd.
Ascot Vale (Melbourne)
VIC 3032

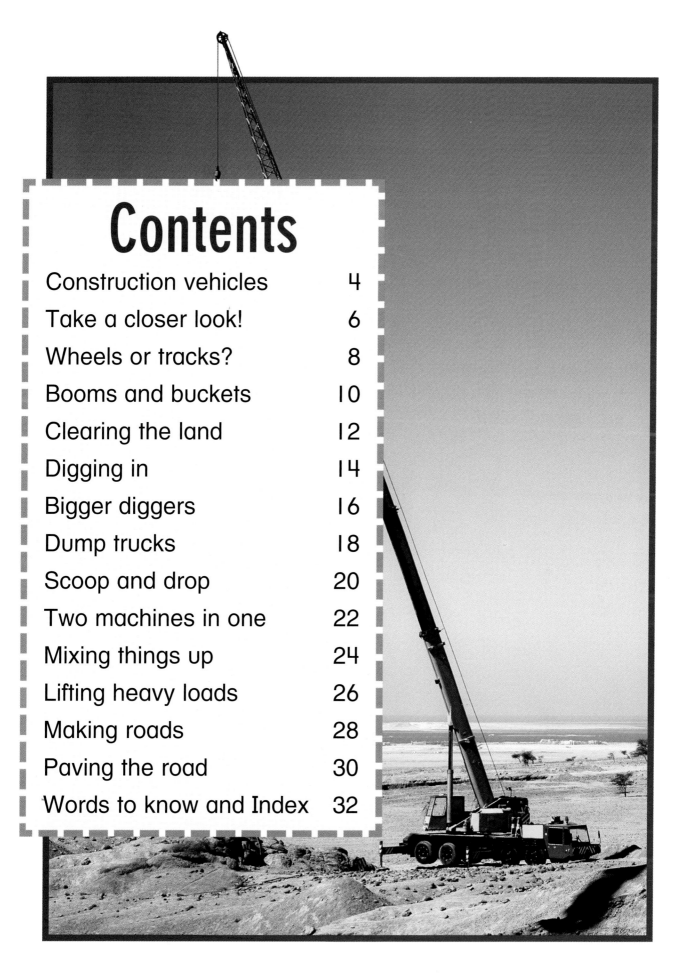

Contents

Construction vehicles

People **construct** roads and buildings. To construct means to build. People use **construction vehicles** to build things. Vehicles are machines that move from place to place. This picture shows construction vehicles.

Tough vehicles

Construction vehicles are tough! Some carry loads of dirt. Others push dirt out of the way. This construction vehicle is a **dump truck**. It carries loads of dirt.

Take a closer look!

Construction vehicles have many parts. Each part does a different job. This construction vehicle is called a **digger**. It digs holes.

*Some construction vehicles have **buckets**. Some buckets dig up dirt. Other buckets lift and carry dirt.*

bucket

A construction vehicle has a **cab**. A worker sits in the cab.

controls

There are **controls** in the cab. The controls move parts of the vehicle. The worker uses the controls.

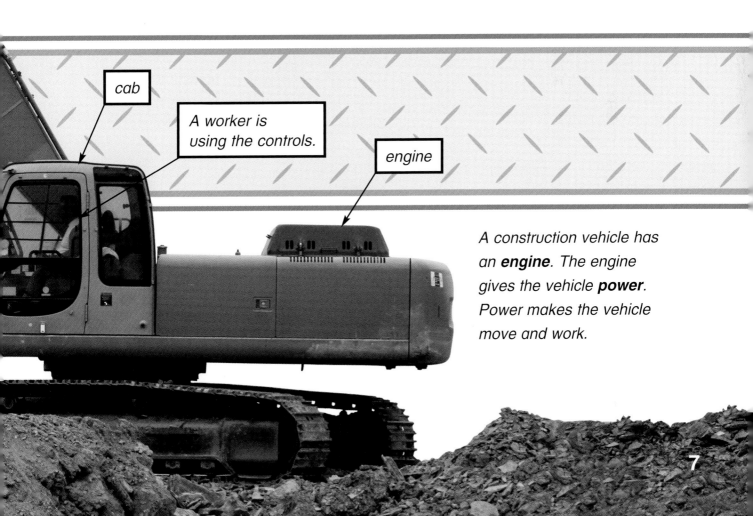

cab

A worker is using the controls.

engine

A construction vehicle has an **engine**. The engine gives the vehicle **power**. Power makes the vehicle move and work.

Wheels or tracks?

Some construction vehicles have **wheels**. Vehicles with wheels move easily on hard dirt. The wheels have thick tires with **treads**. Treads are grooves in the tires. Treads grip the hard ground.

wheel

tread

Tracks are wide and flat

Wheels cannot move easily on loose dirt. They sink into the dirt. Some construction vehicles have **tracks**. Tracks are wide and flat. They do not sink into loose dirt. Construction vehicles with tracks can move over loose dirt.

track

Tracks are very wide!

Booms and buckets

Many construction vehicles have **booms**. Booms are long, strong arms. Workers use controls to move the booms. Booms can move up or down. They can also bend to reach the ground. Diggers have booms.

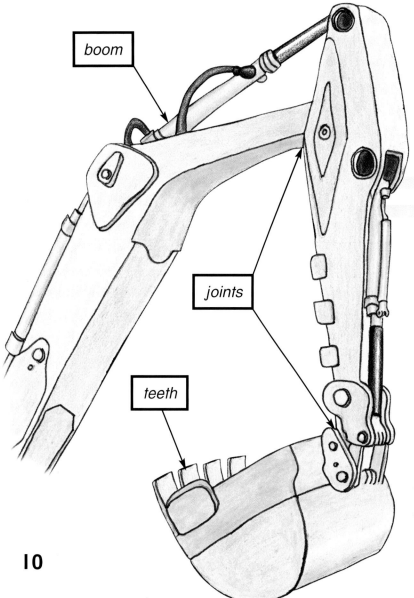

boom

joints

teeth

*A boom has parts called **joints**. Your knees are joints. Joints allow the boom to bend the way your knees bend.*

*Some buckets are made for digging. Most digging buckets have **teeth**. The teeth help dig up dirt.*

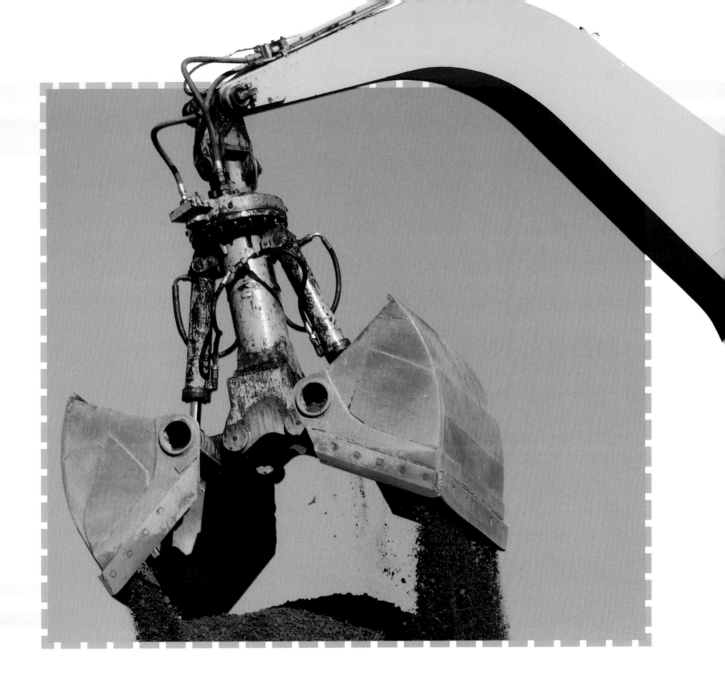

Different buckets

There are different kinds of buckets. This bucket is a **clamshell bucket**. It has two parts. The parts open and close. They open to pick up dirt. They close to carry dirt.

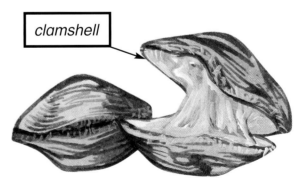

clamshell

A clamshell bucket is named after a clamshell. A clamshell opens and closes.

Clearing the land

A **bulldozer** clears land. It has a **blade**. The blade is on the front of the bulldozer. The blade pushes rocks and dirt out of the way. Then people can build things on the land.

blade

Rip it up

Some bulldozers have **rippers**.
A ripper is a sharp claw. It breaks
hard soil into pieces. The bulldozer's
blade then pushes away
the pieces of soil.

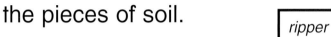

ripper

ripper

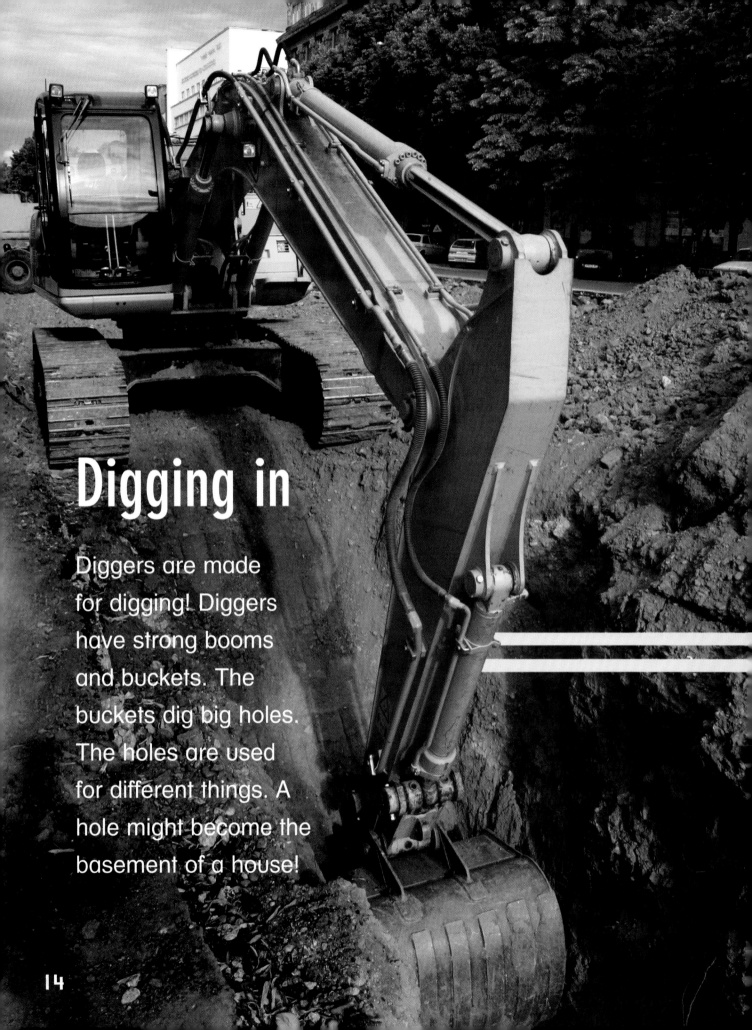

Digging in

Diggers are made for digging! Diggers have strong booms and buckets. The buckets dig big holes. The holes are used for different things. A hole might become the basement of a house!

Moving rocks

Diggers can move heavy rocks. They scoop up rocks in their buckets. They move the rocks out of the way. This picture shows a bucket scooping up some really big rocks.

Bigger diggers

Some diggers are huge!
They dig up rocks in
quarries. Quarries are
big pits filled with rocks.

Big buckets

The bucket on a huge
digger is also very big.
It is big enough to hold
a car! The big bucket can
scoop up a lot of rocks.

Dump trucks

Diggers dig up piles of dirt and rocks. Dump trucks carry the dirt and rocks away. Many dump trucks work at big **construction sites**. A construction site is a place where roads or buildings are made.

back wheels

Dump trucks carry very heavy loads. Most dump trucks have more than two back wheels. These extra wheels help the truck carry heavy loads.

A bed in the back

The back of a dump truck is called the **bed**. A dump truck carries dirt in the bed. The worker in the truck uses the controls to empty the bed. The controls push up the front end of the bed. The dirt slides out when the bed is pushed up.

bed

Scoop and drop

Front-end loaders are construction vehicles that fill dump trucks. They fill dump trucks with dirt and rocks.

Fill and tilt

A front-end loader has a bucket. The bucket moves up and down. It scoops up a load of dirt. The bucket lifts the dirt above the truck. It then tilts forward. The dirt in the bucket falls into the dump truck. The front-end loader keeps dropping dirt into the dump truck. When the bed is full, the dump truck carries the dirt away.

Two machines in one

A **backhoe** is two machines in one! It is a front-end loader. It is also a digger. A backhoe has a large, wide bucket on its front. The bucket scoops up dirt. There is a boom on the back end of a backhoe. The boom has a smaller bucket. The small bucket digs into the ground.

front bucket

back bucket

Backhoes are used in small places. A house is being built in this place.
This backhoe is being used to dig. It also clears away the dirt.

Mixing things up

A **concrete mixer** has a **drum**. The drum is the big round part on the concrete mixer. **Concrete** is mixed in the drum. Concrete is made of sand, gravel, water, and **cement**. Cement makes concrete very hard when it dries.

drum

Concrete is used to make buildings and sidewalks.

Mixing concrete

The drum turns around and around. It turns to mix the concrete. When the concrete is mixed, it pours out of the drum. The concrete pours down a part called the **chute**.

chute

Wet concrete is very soft. It can be spread out. Dry concrete is hard as rock!

Lifting heavy loads

A **crane** is a big machine that lifts. It can lift very heavy objects. Some cranes are **mobile cranes**. Mobile cranes can move from place to place. They move on wheels or tracks. This mobile crane is lifting a big concrete block!

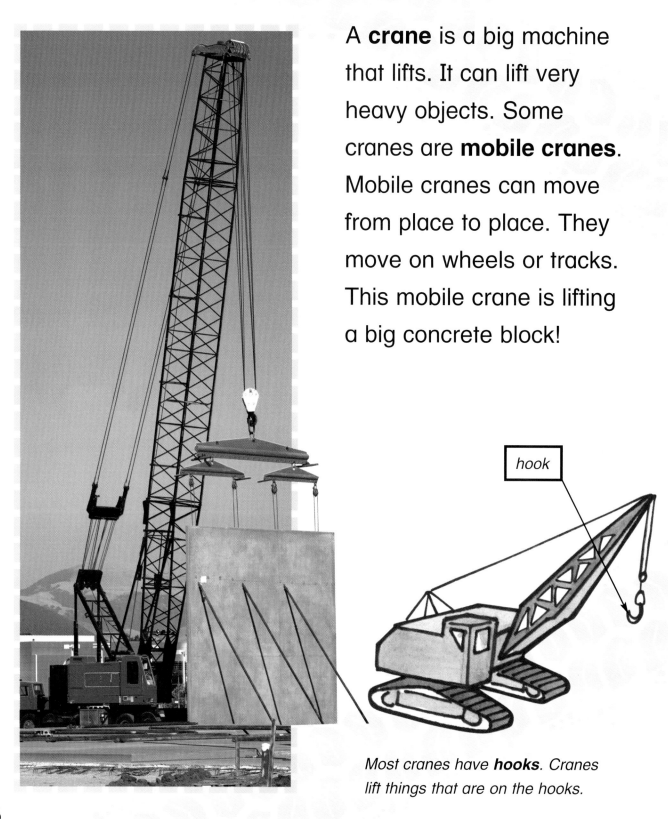

hook

Most cranes have **hooks**. Cranes lift things that are on the hooks.

Holding steady

Most cranes have **legs**. Legs are parts that hold the crane steady. They hold the crane steady while it lifts heavy things.

leg

Making roads

Workers use construction vehicles to construct roads. The first vehicle they use is a **scraper**. It has a blade on its bottom. The blade scrapes bumps off the ground.

This blade is scraping the ground.

Flat ground

Next, a **compactor** drives over the ground. It has heavy, metal tires. The tires make the ground flat.

metal tires

The grader spreads stones with its blade.

Spreading stones

A dump truck dumps stones on the flat ground. A **grader** has a long blade on its bottom. The blade spreads the stones around.

Paving the road

A dump truck dumps **asphalt** into a **road paver**. Asphalt is a sticky liquid. It is mixed with sand or gravel. The road paver spreads the asphalt across the ground. It spreads the asphalt over the stones.

A dump truck dumps asphalt into a road paver.

This road paver is spreading asphalt.

Finishing the job

A **roller** has smooth metal wheels. The roller drives over asphalt. The wheels make the asphalt smooth. The asphalt is very hard when it dries.

The roller has smooth metal wheels.

Words to know and Index

backhoe
pages 22-23

bulldozer
pages 12-13

compactor
page 29

concrete mixer
pages 24-25

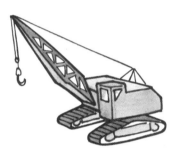

crane
pages 26-27

digger
pages 6, 10,
14-15, 16-17,
18, 22

dump truck
pages 5, 18-19,
20, 29, 30

front-end loader
pages 20-21, 22

grader
page 29

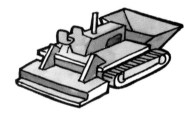

road paver
page 30

roller
page 31

scraper
page 28

Other index words

Printed in the USA